AF599319

Regions of the United States
N
Southwest
by Joanne Mattern
Blastoff! Readers
3
Bellwether Media • Minneapolis, MN

Blastoff! Readers are carefully developed by literacy experts to build reading stamina and move students toward fluency by combining standards-based content with developmentally appropriate text.

Level 1 provides the most support through repetition of high-frequency words, light text, predictable sentence patterns, and strong visual support.

Level 2 offers early readers a bit more challenge through varied sentences, increased text load, and text-supportive special features.

Level 3 advances early-fluent readers toward fluency through increased text load, less reliance on photos, advancing concepts, longer sentences, and more complex special features.

Blastoff! Universe

Reading Level

Grade K

Grades 1–3

Grade 4

This edition first published in 2025 by Bellwether Media, Inc.

Library of Congress Cataloging-in-Publication Data

LC record for Southwest available at: https://lccn.loc.gov/2024039181

Editor: Kieran Downs Designer: Brittany McIntosh

Printed in the United States of America, North Mankato, MN.

Table of Contents

Welcome to the Southwest!

The Southwest is a region of the United States. The region includes four states.

The Southwest was **settled** later than areas in the East and South. The region features many wide-open areas.

States in the Southwest

Arizona
New Mexico
Oklahoma
Texas
N
W
E
S

The Land, Weather, and Wildlife

The Southwest has many deserts. Deep **canyons** cut into the land. Mountains and **plateaus** rise high into the sky.

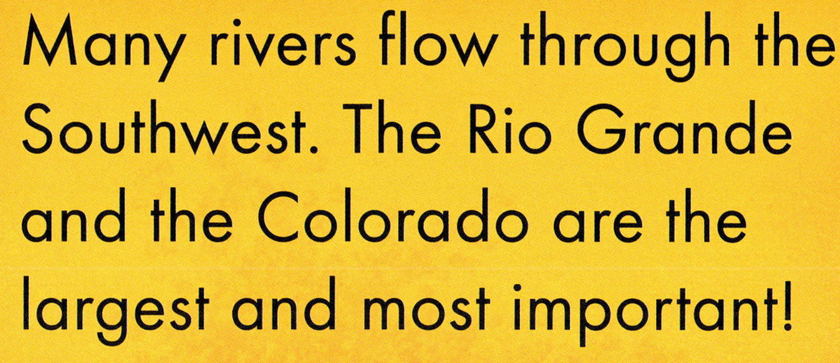

Many rivers flow through the Southwest. The Rio Grande and the Colorado are the largest and most important!

Colorado River

Much of the Southwest has a **semiarid** climate. It is dry and hot. Most places do not get a lot of rain.

In the summer, **temperatures** can be hotter than 100 degrees Fahrenheit (38 degrees Celsius)!

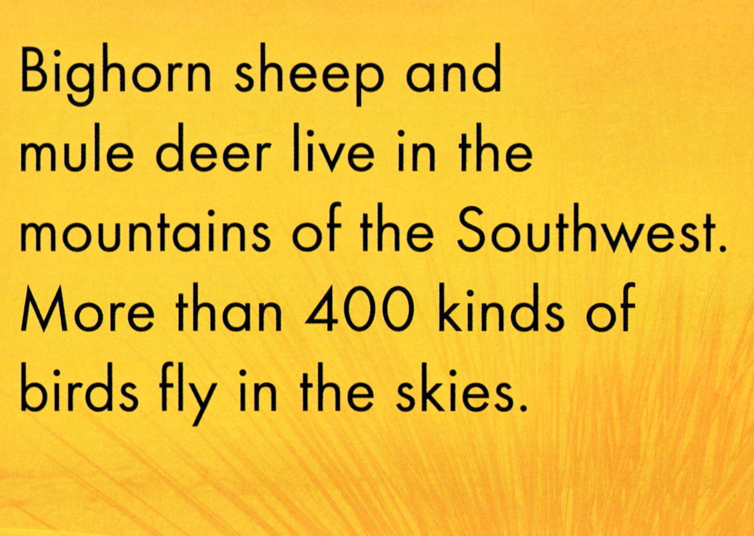

Bighorn sheep and mule deer live in the mountains of the Southwest. More than 400 kinds of birds fly in the skies.

mule deer

Small **mammals**, like prairie dogs, live in the deserts. Rattlesnakes and lizards also call the deserts home.

Natural Resources and Industry

Farmers in the Southwest grow many crops. Others raise animals. There is plenty of land for **grazing**.

Agriculture

land to graze

farmers raise animals

copper mine

People mine gold, silver, and copper in the Southwest. **Tourism** is an important **industry**, too.

People of the Southwest

Many people with Native American **ancestors** live in the Southwest. Others have European or Hispanic ancestors.

Most people in the Southwest live in **urban** areas. Houston, Texas, is the largest city in the region.

Houston, Texas

Food is an important part of Southwestern **culture**. People enjoy Mexican favorites. These include tacos and burritos.

tacos

Green chile peppers, beans, and corn are common in Southwestern food. People put them in many dishes.

People in the Southwest love to be outdoors. There are many places to hike, bike, and camp.

Southwesterners enjoy many festivals. Thousands visit the Texas State Fair. Others enjoy art or music festivals. There is always fun in the Southwest!

Texas State Fair

Places to Visit
Painted Desert
Arizona
Alamogordo, New Mexico
The Alamo
San Antonio, Texas
N
W
E
S
White Sands National Park

Southwest Fast Facts

3 Largest Cities (2020)

1

Houston, Texas

Population: around 2.3 million

2

Phoenix, Arizona

Population: around 1.6 million

3

San Antonio, Texas

Population: around 1.4 million

State Populations (2020)

Arizona 7.1 million

New Mexico 2.1 million

Oklahoma 4 million

Texas 29.1 million

Major Sports Teams

Houston Astros

(MLB)

Arizona Cardinals

(NFL)

Oklahoma City Thunder

(NBA)

Famous Face

Name: Beyoncé
Hometown: Houston, Texas
Famous for: Top-selling musical artist and actress

Smallest State

Oklahoma
69,899 square miles
(181,038 square kilometers)

Largest State

Texas
268,596 square miles
(695,660 square kilometers)

Glossary

ancestors–relatives who lived long ago

canyons–deep, narrow valleys with steep sides

culture–the beliefs, arts, and ways of life in a place or society

grazing–eating grass or other plants that are growing in a field or pasture

industry–a group of businesses that provide a certain product or service

mammals–warm-blooded animals that have backbones and feed their young milk

plateaus–areas of high, flat ground

semiarid–related to a climate that is mostly dry with little rainfall

settled–filled with people who moved to live in a new place

temperatures–measurements of how cold or hot something is

tourism–the business of people traveling to visit other places

urban–related to cities or city life

To Learn More

AT THE LIBRARY

Gagne, Tammy. *Texas*. Minneapolis, Minn.: Abdo Publishing, 2023.

Larsen, Ib. *Arizona*. Minneapolis, Minn.: Abdo Publishing, 2024.

Spanier, Kristine. *Explore the Southwest*. Minneapolis, Minn.: Jump!, 2023.

ON THE WEB

FACTSURFER

Factsurfer.com gives you a safe, fun way to find more information.

1. Go to www.factsurfer.com.
2. Enter "Southwest" into the search box and click .
3. Select your book cover to see a list of related content.

Index

The images in this book are reproduced through the courtesy of: LouieLea, front cover (main), p. 9; Serge Yatunin, front cover (bottom left); Sean Pavone, front cover (bottom center), pp. 6, 20 (Houston); EWY Media, front cover (bottom right); boommaval, p. 3; Zack Frank, pp. 4, 19 (White Sands National Park); ON-Photography Germany, p. 7; 86Eric_Anthony_Mischke 86, p. 8; Rachel Portwood, p. 10; Warren Price Photography, p. 11 (top); Clint H, p. 11 (bottom); BUI LE MANH HUNG, p. 12 (left); Fotoluminate LLC, p. 12 (right); Phil Degginger/ Alamy, p. 13; Trong Nguyen, p. 14; Nate Hovee, p. 15; Alex Borderline, p. 16; Ravi Bhor Photography, p. 17 (top); Ozgur Senergin, p. 17 (bottom); fdastidillo, p. 18; Eric Poulin, pp. 18-19; The Old Major, p. 19 (Painted Desert); Kokoulina, p. 19 (The Alamo); Kevin Ruck, p. 20 (Phoenix); Jacob Boomsma, p. 20 (San Antonio); Houston Astros/ Wikipedia, p. 21 (Astros logo); Arizona Cardinals/ Wikipedia, p. 21 (Cardinals logo); Oklahoma City Thunder/ Wikipedia, p. 21 (Thunder logo); Kevin Mazur/ Contributor/ Getty, p. 21 (Beyoncé); Eric Isselee, p. 23.